Kenya

Sean McCollum

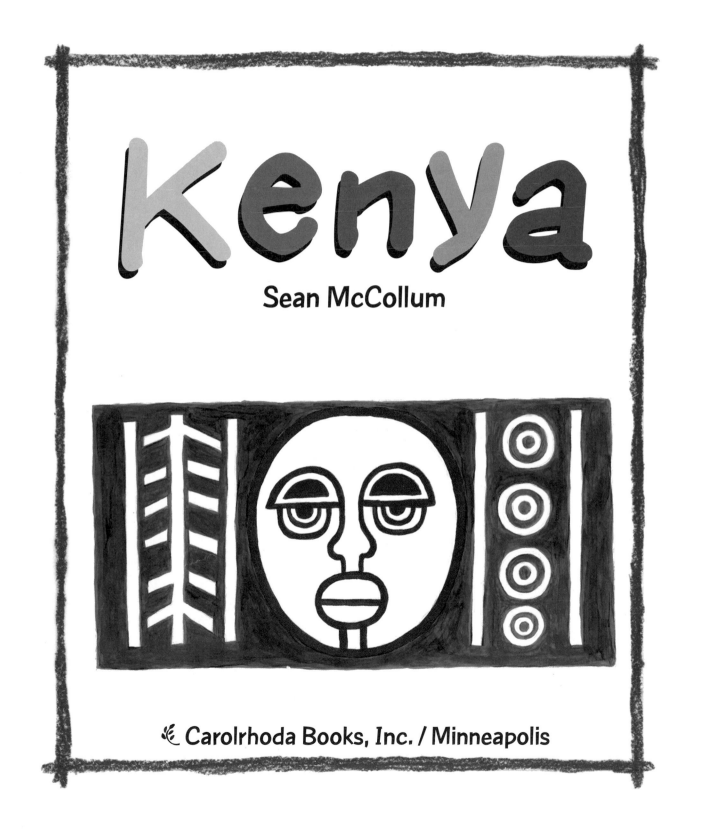

Carolrhoda Books, Inc. / Minneapolis

Photo Acknowledgments

Photos, maps, and artwork are used courtesy of: John Erste, pp. 1, 2–3, 9, 18–19, 21, 25, 27, 35, 42; Laura Westlund, pp. 4, 29; © Phil Porter, pp. 6 (left), 19, 27, 43 (left); © Jason Laure, pp. 6 (right), 7, 13 (left and right), 14, 15 (bottom), 17, 18, 26, 28, 29 (bottom), 33 (left), 36 (top and bottom), 39 (left), 41; © Michele Burgess, pp. 8, 9 (left and right), 15 (top) 23, 25 (bottom), 30, 34, 37, 40, 43 (right); © James P. Rowan, pp. 10–11, 12, 16 (left and right), 20 (top), 29 (top), 44; UPI/Bettmann, p. 11; © David F. Clobes/photo by Sue Kelm, p. 20 (bottom), 24; © Eugene G. Schultz, pp. 22, 32; © Frank Balthis, pp. 25 (top), 38, 39 (right); © September 8th Stock, Walt/Louiseann Pietrowicz, p. 31; © Liba Taylor, p. 33. Cover photo of kids © Michele Burgess.

Carolrhoda Books, Inc.
A Division of the Lerner Publishing Group
241 First Avenue North
Minneapolis, Minnesota 55401 U.S.A.

Website address: www.lernerbooks.com

Library of Congress Cataloging-in-Publication Data

McCollum, Sean.
Kenya / by Sean McCollum.
   p. cm. — (A ticket to)
   Includes bibliographical references and index.
   Summary: Discusses the people, geography, religion, languages, customs, lifestyle, and culture of Kenya.
   ISBN 1–57505–130–3 (lib. bdg. : alk. paper)
   1. Kenya—Juvenile literature. [1. Kenya.] I. Title. II. Series.
DT433.522.M43 1999   98–36632
967.62—dc21

Manufactured in the United States of America
2 3 4 5 6 7 – JR – 04 03 02 01 00 99

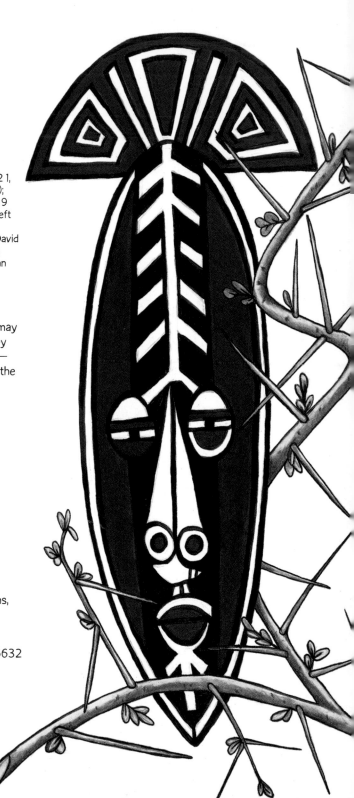

Contents

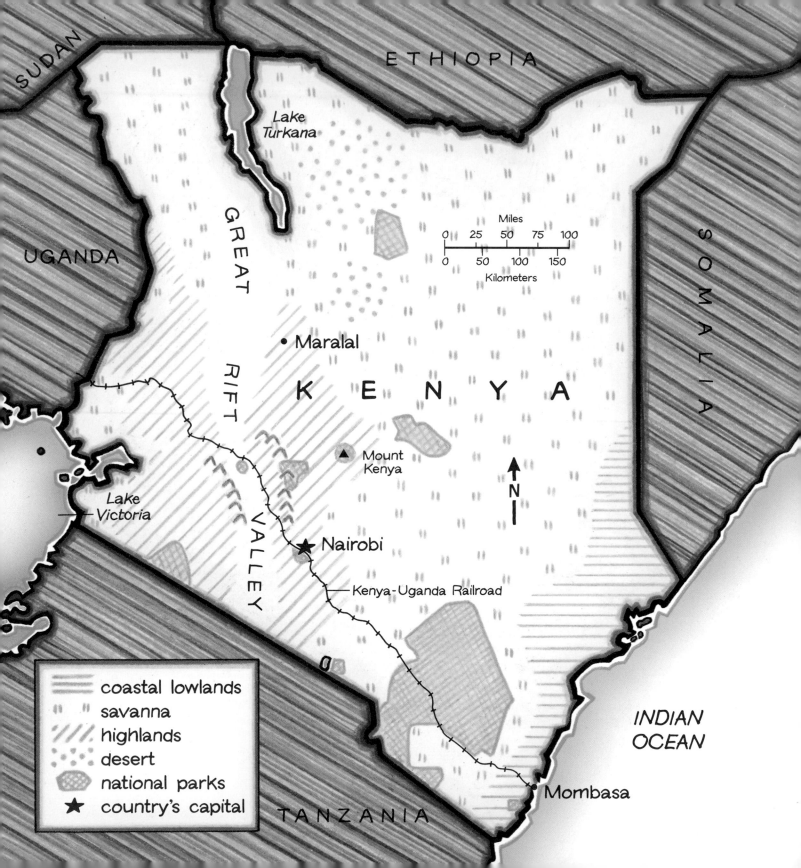

SUDAN

ETHIOPIA

UGANDA

SOMALIA

*Lake
Turkana*

G
R
E
A
T

R
I
F
T

V
A
L
L
E
Y

• Maralal

K E N Y A

▲ Mount
Kenya

Lake
Victoria

N

★ Nairobi

Kenya-Uganda Railroad

Miles

0   25   50   75   100

0   50   100   150

Kilometers

INDIAN
OCEAN

Mombasa

TANZANIA

coastal lowlands
savanna
highlands
desert
national parks
★ country's capital

Welcome!

To find the country of Kenya on a map, locate the **continent** of Africa and look for the biggest lake. That body of water is Lake Victoria, which touches Kenya's southwestern edge. The Indian Ocean meets Kenya's eastern side. This African nation does not have seasons—spring, summer, autumn, and winter—like North America does. Instead, Kenya has wet and dry seasons. When it does not rain for a long time, some lakes and rivers dry up. They fill again when the rains come.

Steep mountains (left) *rise from Kenya's highlands. Sandy beaches* (above) *are great places to cool off in the hot lowlands.*

Highs and Lows

Southwestern Kenya has **mountain ranges** and deep **valleys.** This part of Kenya, called the highlands, gets cool weather. The **lowlands** near the Indian Ocean have hot weather. What do these regions have in common? Lots of rain and lots of people. Most Kenyans are farmers and need water to raise crops. What is between the highlands and the lowlands? The **savanna**—dry grasslands.

A group of giraffes gallops through the Kenyan savanna—a dry, grassy area that is home to many types of animals.

Map Whiz Quiz

Take a look at the map on page four. A map is a drawing or chart of a place. Trace the outline of Kenya on a piece of paper. Do you see the Indian Ocean on the map? Mark this side of your paper with an "E" for east. Find the country of Uganda. Write a "W" for west on that side. Color Kenya green. Choose another crayon to color the five countries that touch Kenya.

Nap time! A lioness and her cubs relax in the savanna. These hunters often sleep for up to 20 hours a day.

Land of Animals

Grab your camera! We're going on a **safari** to see Kenya's wild animals. As the truck bounces over the savanna, you might spot lions, giraffes, and elephants. Did you hear something walking through the grass? It could be a zebra, a leopard, or a rhinoceros.

A Baboon Stole My Camera!

At a hotel in one of Kenya's national parks, baboons (fierce monkeys) sometimes sneak into open windows. Guests take a risk if they leave a camera or other small items laying on their dresser or bed. A baboon might take them!

Click

Visitors to Kenya can snap pictures of elephants (left) *and giraffes* (below) *while on a safari.*

Early Peoples

Members of more than 40 **ethnic groups** live in Kenya. The people of an ethnic group share a religion, a history, and a language. Kenyan languages are a lot like the languages people speak in other parts of Africa. That is because long ago groups of Africans from the west, north, and northeast moved to

Thousands of years ago, Kenya's super farmland drew settlers from western, northern, and northeastern Africa. They are the long-ago relatives of modern-day Kenyans.

what would become Kenya. These newcomers pushed out or joined the people who were already living there.

Old Bones

In the Great Rift Valley in western Kenya, scientists discovered some bones that are millions of years old. No kidding! They think these skeletons may be from human ancestors, which would mean that our earliest relatives lived in East Africa. That is how the region got the nickname "the cradle of humanity."

In the late 1500s, the Portuguese ruled the eastern coast of Africa. They built this huge fort in the coastal city of Mombasa.

Many Peoples

The long-ago relatives of almost all Kenyans came from other parts of Africa. But people whose families arrived from other continents are also mixed into the nation's **population.** Centuries ago Arabs settled along the coast of the Indian Ocean.

In 1895 Britain took control of East Africa, including what has become Kenya. During British rule, Indians came to help lay railroad tracks in Kenya and many stayed.

Long-ago Arab traders introduced dhows (left)—a type of sailboat—to Kenyan sailors. These Indians (above) are related to people who came to Kenya from India in the early 1900s.

This woman is a member of the Kikuyu, the largest ethnic group in Kenya.

Who Are You?

The way Kenyans live depends a lot on whether their long-ago relatives settled in the highlands, in the savanna, or on the coast. In some villages, the people are expert farmers or fishers. Talented craftspeople live in other locations. In parts of Kenya, groups of herders move from place to place to find food and water

One or Many?

Kenyan leaders want citizens to practice *harambee*. This word means "all pull together" in Kiswahili, a widely used Kenyan language. But many people want to keep ties with their age-old way of life. Sometimes it is hard for Kenyans with very different histories to work together.

This boy (above) *comes from the Samburu ethnic group, whose members move from place to place with their animals. Many Luo people* (below) *fish the waters of Lake Victoria.*

for their animals. Traders and people who work for the government or businesses often live in the cities.

Big City

Nairobi is the **capital** of Kenya and the nation's largest city. People from all over the country come to live or to sell their goods in the capital. Like other Kenyan cities, Nairobi has electricity. Having lights makes it

A building constructed during British rule (left) shares the Nairobi skyline with this modern structure (above).

Population Boom

The population in Kenya is growing fast. Many young adults *(above)* who cannot get land move to Nairobi to find work. Builders cannot keep up with the numbers of people that arrive. So some people use scraps of metal and cardboard to build their homes.

possible for city folks to stay out past dark. After work people in Nairobi may head for a restaurant, a movie theater, or a dance club.

On the Move

Few Kenyans own cars. People take buses and trains, walk, or ride in vans called *matatus.* Matatu

All aboard! Kenyans squeeze into a matatu.

drivers charge low fares to take people to out-of-the-way villages, but they squeeze in many riders. You might even share your seat with a chicken or a goat when someone needs to move animals they just bought! Hang on tight because drivers speed down Kenya's bumpy roads!

On Track

Kenya's highland farmers load their tea, coffee, and produce onto trains headed for the coast. Then workers put the goods on ships that carry them to other parts of the world.

Village Life

The round homes in this Kikuyu village (above) *were built with branches and grass. A Kenyan woman* (right) *carries a load of sweet potatoes on her head.*

Do you know anyone who lives on a farm? Most Kenyans live in farming villages. Village kids sure have busy days! They help their moms raise food, cook meals, wash clothes, and carry water from the well. Older children baby-sit their younger brothers and sisters. And that is not all. Many kids go to school, too. But when chores are done, village kids make time to horse around.

The Movie Truck

Many Kenyan villages do not have electricity. So the government sometimes sends a truck with a machine that makes electricity. The driver also brings movies, a projector, and a screen. Show time!

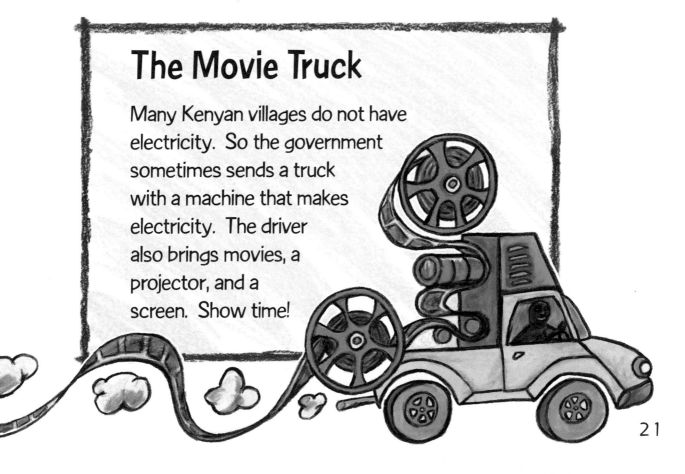

Family

When Kenyan kids talk about family, they mean aunts, uncles, cousins, and grandparents, too. Most kids have more than five brothers and

All in the Family

Here are the Kiswahili words and pronunciations for family members. Practice them on your own family. See if they understand you!

grandfather	*babu*	(BAH-boo)
grandmother	*nyanya*	(NYAH-nyah)
father	*baba*	(BAH-bah)
mother	*mama*	(MAH-mah)
uncle	*mjomba*	(mm-JOHM-bah)
aunt	*mbiomba*	(mm-bee-OHM-bah)
son	*bin*	(BEEN)
daughter	*binti*	(BEEN-tee)
brother	*ndugu*	(nn-DOO-goo)
sister	*dada*	(DAH-dah)

Kids often have many brothers and sisters, so Kenyan villages have lots of children.

sisters. Kenyan tradition says a man can have as many wives as he can afford. So some kids have lots of half brothers and half sisters. These days more men marry just one woman.

Home Sweet Home

Some Kenyans live in modern apartments or houses with plumbing and electricity. But in many villages, families build homes from what they find nearby. They construct walls from branches and a mixture of grass and mud. To make a snug roof, Kenyans weave

palm leaves or grass. In some homes, grown-ups cannot stand straight because the ceilings are just five feet high!

Kenyans build their homes from all sorts of material. Some farmhouses (facing page) are made of wood, mud, and grass. Near Nairobi (top), brick houses are common. A Masai woman (above) adds some mud to the roof of her home.

Do Not Waste a Drop!

If a village does not have running water, kids and their moms must carry heavy containers from wells—sometimes for several miles. Other families can afford to pay someone to deliver jugs of water.

English is Kenya's official language. Do you recognize some of the words on these posters?

Shared Language

Each ethnic group in Kenya has its own language. In villages or when city folks are at home, Kenyans use the language of their relatives. But lots of Kenyans learn Kiswahili so they can understand one another when

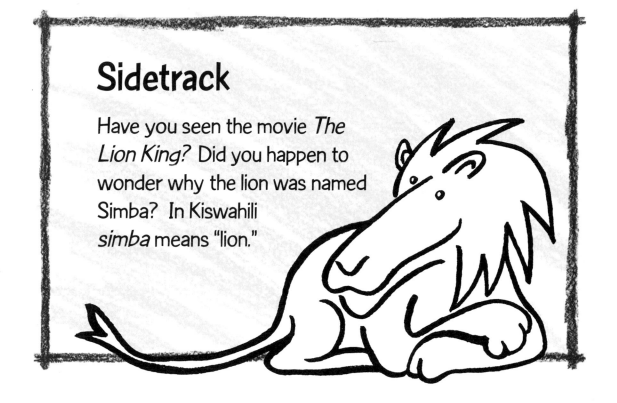

Sidetrack

Have you seen the movie *The Lion King?* Did you happen to wonder why the lion was named Simba? In Kiswahili *simba* means "lion."

they meet at the market, at school, or at work. In fact, Kiswahili is Kenya's national language. English is the official language, which Kenyans use for government and international business. Kenyan kids study English in high school.

Religions

Some Kenyans follow ancient African religions, which teach that spirits live in rocks, trees, and animals. But many ethnic groups mix these beliefs with

A Christian wedding in Kenya (above). *Kenyan Muslims worship in mosques* (facing page, top).

Christianity. More than half of Kenyans are Christians. Arabs brought the Islamic religion to Africa. In some coastal cities, many Kenyans are Muslims (followers of Islam). Kenya's **ethnic Indians** practice Hinduism— a religion their families brought from India.

Dear Grandma and Grandpa,

Today we sailed on the Indian Ocean. Dad said Mombasa, the city where we are staying, is a big port. That means huge ships can drop off and pick up goods. (Whoops, I forgot to tell you the city is on an island.) Many people in Mombasa are Muslims. Even though it is hot, Muslim women wear outfits called *buibuis*—long black dresses and head coverings. And guess what else! The roofs of mosques—the buildings where Muslims worship—look just like onions.

See you soon!

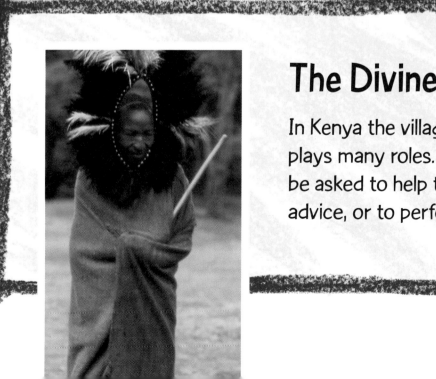

The Diviner

In Kenya the village diviner often plays many roles. The diviner may be asked to help the sick, to give advice, or to perform magic.

29

Good Food

If you ask Kenyan kids, "What do you eat?" a lot of them will answer *ugali,* a cornmeal porridge. Families also eat other foods they grow on their *shamba* (farm), including millet, wheat, rice, cassava, sweet potatoes, and

vegetables. Popular fruits are mangoes, papayas, pineapples, and plantains (a type of banana). People who live near water

Irio, *a dish that includes potatoes, corn, and peas, is a Kenyan favorite.*

eat fish. Kenyans—even those who raise cows, sheep, or goats—eat little meat.

Baked Plantains

Kenyans cook plantains in many ways. If you lived in the Kenyan highlands, you would probably pick the fruit just before you bake it. Ask a grown-up to help you prepare this dessert, which makes enough for four people.

You will need:
4 large, ripe plantains
½ cup brown sugar
¾ teaspoon cinnamon
¼ cup butter or margarine, melted

1. *Preheat oven to 350°F.*
2. *Wash plantains and cut them in half lengthwise. Do not peel.*
3. *Arrange plantains in a shallow baking dish with cut sides facing up.*
4. *In a small bowl, combine brown sugar, cinnamon, and melted butter. Stir well.*
5. *Pour brown sugar mixture over the plantains.*
6. *Cover pan and bake for 35 minutes or until plantains are soft.*
7. *Remove from oven and let cool slightly before serving.*

School Time

Most Kenyan kids start elementary school when they are six years old. A lot of schools run all year, but students get vacations during March, July, and November. Youngsters wear school uniforms and study Kiswahili, math, geography, science, and agriculture.

Education is very important to Kenyans. Students in Kenyan high schools (left) *and colleges* (facing page) *study hard.*

Parents must pay money for kids to go to high school. Many families cannot afford to send all of their children. So at age 14, teenagers often set off to work.

A Girl from the Coast

Meet 11-year-old Salaama Katama. She lives in the town of Magogoni. Salaama goes to an elementary school in nearby Mombasa. She studies hard so she will pass the tough test to get into high school.

This monument in Nairobi (left) celebrates Kenyan independence. Each color in the Kenyan flag (below) has a special meaning. Black stands for Kenya's people, red makes Kenyans remember how hard they worked for freedom, and green stands for farming. The shield and spears show that Kenyans plan to stay free.

Celebrate!

On December 12, 1963, Kenya became a free nation. Each year city dwellers celebrate with huge parades. Musicians and dancers wear fancy costumes. Many people return to their home villages to spend the day with relatives.

Religious holidays are important to Kenyans. Christmas and Easter mean the most for Christians. During the month of Ramadan, Muslims do not eat or drink from dawn until sunset. The food served at the festival that follows Ramadan sure tastes good.

Are you ready for a crazy day? Head to the Kenyan highlands for the Maralal International Camel Derby. Have you heard the expression "spitting mad"? These stubborn camels may spit or kneel down instead of racing.

People in Kenya love sports. Kenyan long-distance runners (left) *are some of the best in the world. Kenyan soccer players* (below) *show off some fancy footwork.*

Sports and Games

On your mark. Get set. Go! Kenya's runners are fast. They won eight medals for Kenya in the 1996 Summer Olympics. But Kenyans also enjoy team sports. Their favorite game is soccer, which they call football.

36

When Kenyan kids are not racing across the savanna or kicking a soccer ball, they try to beat one another at checkers or in a board game called *kigogo.*

Two Kenyans enjoy a game of kigogo.

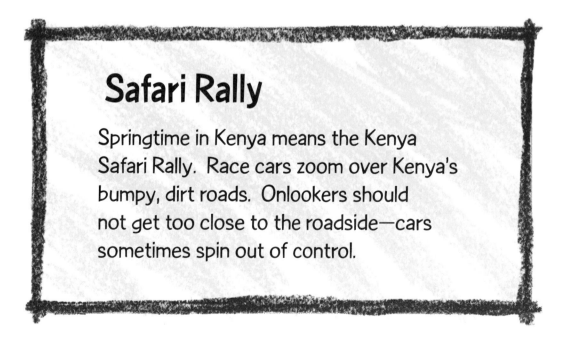

Safari Rally

Springtime in Kenya means the Kenya Safari Rally. Race cars zoom over Kenya's bumpy, dirt roads. Onlookers should not get too close to the roadside—cars sometimes spin out of control.

Boing! These Samburu men are performing a special dance where they jump as high they can.

Dance and Music

Traditional dances for births, weddings, and funerals make these events even more special for Kenyans. Long-ago people wrote music to go along with the dances.

But these days Kenyan musicians mix age-old African sounds with music from around the world, such as rock and roll.

Watch a Kenyan band and you may see one member playing a hand-carved African drum while another musician strums an electric guitar.

Kenyans of all ages love music. In Nairobi children (left) take part in music competitions. This group of Kenyan street musicians (above) makes music with old guitars and homemade instruments.

The colorful, beaded jewelry made by Kenya's Masai people is known around the world.

Everyday Art

Kenyans like to make everyday objects beautiful. Some folks skillfully dye fabrics. Other people create jewelry from colorful beads or metal.

Carving, too, is an age-old Kenyan skill. Craftspeople make drums, dance masks, and stools from wood. Under the knives of expert Kenyan carvers, a smooth rock called Kisii stone becomes small statues of animals.

This Kenyan artist is putting the finishing touches on a wooden statue.

Story Time

Sikilizeni hadithi yangu means "listen to my story" in Kiswahili. Kenyans love to spend the evening gathered around a good storyteller.

Sneaky Rabbit

Have you heard of Bre'r Rabbit? This critter always wins because he plays tricks on stronger animals. Did you know that the stories about Bre'r Rabbit came from Africa? In Kenya the rabbit has many names. In one Kenyan language, the word for rabbit means "the one that sleeps while his eyes are open."

Musicians sometimes play wooden flutes (left) as a storyteller weaves a tale. Kenyan stories often contain several types of animals, such as the leopard (below).

Animal tales are popular. The person telling the story creates a special voice for each creature. Get cozy! A good storyteller can go on for hours.

Mount Kenya, the country's tallest mountain, is the second-highest mountain in Africa.

New Words to Learn

capital: A city where the government is located.

continent: Any one of seven large areas of land. The continents are Africa, Antarctica, Asia, Australia, Europe, North America, and South America.

ethnic group: A group of people with many things in common, such as language, religion, and customs.

ethnic Indian: A person whose ethnic group is from India.

44

lowland: A region that is lower than the surrounding land.

mountain range: A series, or group, of mountains—the parts of the earth's surface that rise high into the sky.

population: The total number of people living in an area, such as a nation or a city.

safari: A journey, often in Africa.

savanna: A tropical grassland.

valley: A low-lying piece of land between hills or mountains. Valley can also mean an area of land that gets its water from a large river.

Sidetrack

Some folks in Kenya feel that it is rude to eat inside. If families have meals outdoors, they can invite passersby to join them!

New Words to Say

buibui	boo-ee-BOO-ee
harambee	hah-RAHM-bay
irio	ee-REE-oh
kigogo	kee-GOH-goh
Kisii	KEE-see
Kiswahili	kee-swah-HEE-lee
Magogoni	mah-goh-GOH-nee
matatu	mah-TAH-too
Mombasa	mohm-BAH-sah
mosque	MAHSK
Nairobi	ny-ROH-bee
Ramadan	RAH-muh-dahn
Salaama Katama	sah-LAH-mah kah-TAH-mah
shamba	SHAHM-bah
sikilizeni	see-kee-lee-ZAY-nee
hadithi	haw-DEE-thee
yangu	YAHNG-goo
simba	SIHM-bah
ugali	oo-GAH-lee

More Books to Read

Ferber, Elizabeth. *A Life with Animals: Jane Goodall.* New York: Benchmark Books, 1997.

Griffin, Michael. *A Family in Kenya.* Minneapolis: Lerner Publications Company, 1988.

Hanna, Jack and Rick A. Prebeg. *Jungle Jack Hanna's Safari Adventure.* New York: Scholastic, 1996.

Haskins, Jim. *Count Your Way through Africa.* Minneapolis: Carolrhoda Books, Inc., 1989.

Kituku, Dr. Vincent Muli Wa. *East African Folktales: From the Voice of Mukamba.* Little Rock, AK: August House, 1997.

MacMillan, Dianne M. *Cheetahs.* Minneapolis: Carolrhoda Books, Inc., 1997.

Sammis, Fran. *Colors of Kenya.* Minneapolis: Carolrhoda Books, Inc., 1998.

Silver, Donald M. *African Savanna.* New York: Scientific American Books for Young Readers, 1994.

Smith, Roland. *African Elephants.* Minneapolis: Lerner Publications Company, 1995.

Stelson, Caren Barzelay. *Safari.* Minneapolis: Carolrhoda Books, Inc., 1988.

Temko, Florence. *Traditional Crafts from Africa.* Minneapolis: Lerner Publications Company, 1996.

Walker, Sally M. *Rhinos.* Minneapolis: Carolrhoda Books, Inc., 1996.

New Words to Find